Pilots and Flights

By Cameron Macintosh

A pilot is someone who can fly a plane.

Pilots can fly in the daylight, and they can fly at night.

This pilot can fly a big plane.

Big planes can take lots of us a long way.

This pilot has a black tie.

The pilot takes this big plane into the sky.

It is quite a sight!

Big planes fly very high in the sky.

Kylee sighs at the sights on the flight.

She likes what she sees.

Big planes need two pilots.

But this pilot can fly a small plane by himself.

Small planes cannot fly as high in the sky as big planes.

This plane glides.
It floats in the sky!

This type of plane cannot get into the sky by itself.

This type of plane is pulled up high by a rope.

When the rope drops, the plane glides in the sky.

Dad takes Eve's hand.
She got a fright on the flight.

But it is safe!

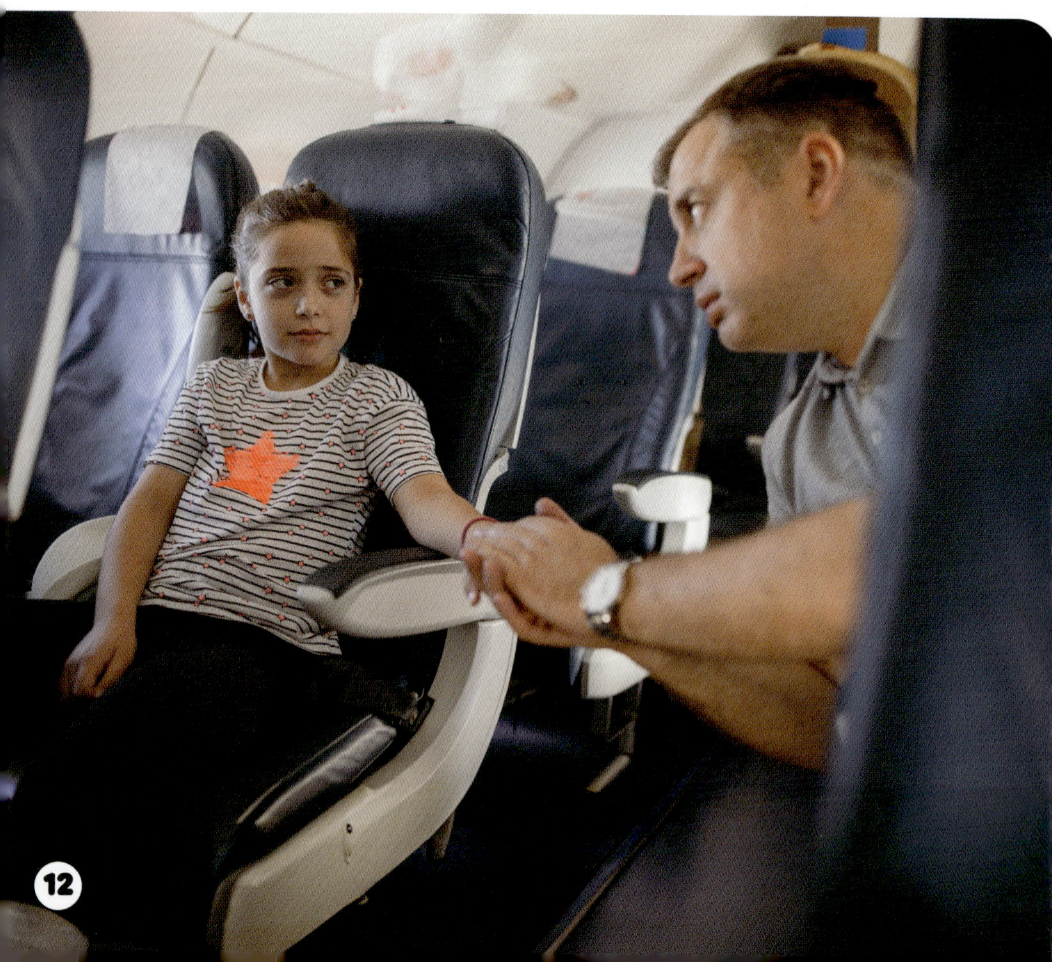

I can be a pilot
and fly a little plane!

I can make a plane to fly.

CHECKING FOR MEANING

1. Can pilots fly when it is dark? *(Literal)*
2. What are two differences between big planes and small planes? *(Literal)*
3. Why does a gliding plane need another plane to pull it into the sky? *(Inferential)*

EXTENDING VOCABULARY

daylight	What two words make up the word *daylight*? How do those two words help you understand the meaning of the word?
sight	Which letters in the word *sight* make the long /ī/ sound? How does the word *sight* relate to the word *see*?
high	Read the word *high*. How many letters does this word have? How many sounds? What is the opposite of *high*?

MOVING BEYOND THE TEXT

1. Flying in a plane is one way to travel from one place to another. What are some other ways we can travel?
2. Have you ever been on a plane? If you have, tell me about it. If you haven't, where would you like to go on a plane?
3. What things might you see from a plane in the sky? How would the view be different from when you are standing on the ground?
4. Would you rather fly in a big plane, a small plane or a gliding plane? Why?

TIME TO WRITE

Write about which of the planes in this book you would most like to fly in. Explain why.

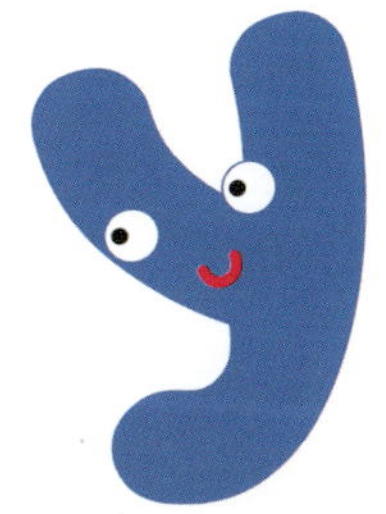

PRACTICE WORDS

pilot

fly

daylight

night

pilots

sight

sighs

sky

I

fright

sights

tie

by

high

flight

Kylee